Korean Heritage
Celebrating Diversity in My Classroom

By Tamra B. Orr

21st Century
Junior Library

Published in the United States of America by
Cherry Lake Publishing
Ann Arbor, Michigan
www.cherrylakepublishing.com

Reading Adviser: Marla Conn MS, Ed., Literacy specialist, Read-Ability, Inc.

Photo Credits: © yut photo / Shutterstock Images, cover; © Sanga Park / Shutterstock Images, 4, 18; © Yein Jeon / Shutterstock Images, 6; © wizdata / Shutterstock Images, 8; © Urn Run / Shutterstock Images, 10; © oerb / Shutterstock Images, 12; © Eun / Shutterstock Images, 14; © Victor Jiang / Shutterstock Images, 16; © yochika photographer / Shutterstock Images, 20

Library of Congress Cataloging-in-Publication Data
Name: Orr, Tamra, author.
Title: Korean heritage / by Tamra B. Orr.
Description: Ann Arbor : Cherry Lake Publishing, 2018. | Series: Celebrating diversity in my classroom | Includes bibliographical references and index.
Identifiers: LCCN 2017035948 | ISBN 9781534107403 (hardcover) | ISBN 9781534109384 (pdf) | ISBN 9781534108394 (pbk.) | ISBN 9781534120372 (hosted ebook)
Subjects: LCSH: Korea (South)—Social life and customs—Juvenile literature.
Classification: LCC DS907.4 .O77 2018 | DDC 951.95—dc23
LC record available at https://lccn.loc.gov/2017035948

Cherry Lake Publishing would like to acknowledge the work of The Partnership for 21st Century Skills.
Please visit *www.p21.org* for more information.

Printed in the United States of America
Corporate Graphics

CONTENTS

The capital of South Korea is Seoul.

Super South Korea

Korea is the **peninsula** between China and Japan. Unlike most countries, Korea is split in half.

South Korea is about the size of Kentucky. Yet almost 50 million people live there! People from South Korea have also **emigrated** to other countries. There are about 1 million **immigrants** from South Korea in the United States! What is their home country like? Read ahead to find out!

People from Korea also bow when saying thank you or excuse me.

Ya! Ch'in-gu!

Did you hear someone from South Korea shout, *"Ya! Ch'in-gu!"*? It means, "Hey friend!" Chances are this person would also bow to you. In South Korea, handshakes are not used as often as the bow. Good friends bow to each other. So do strangers.

All Koreans speak the same language. Korean is a difficult language for many Americans to learn. Many Korean words

Traditional Korean kites are rectangular with a hole in the middle.

tend to sound the same. For example, here is a Korean tongue twister:

"Kanjang kongjang kongjang-jang-un jang kongjang-jang-igo

doenjang kongjang kongjang-jang-un kang kongjang-jang-ida!"

What does this mean? "The factory manager of the soy sauce factory is factory manager Chang. And the factory manager of the soybean paste factory is factory manager Kang."

Many Buddhists practice mindfulness, or being present in each moment.

Following a Wise Man

There is more than one religion in South Korea. About one-quarter of the people are Christian. Another quarter are **Buddhist**. The remaining half have other religious beliefs.

A number of South Koreans follow a way of life called **Confucianism**. This is not so much a religion. It is more a way of thinking and behaving. It is based on the teachings of a wise Chinese man named Confucius.

The Munmyo Ilmu dance is part of a ceremony celebrating Confucius every year.

People who follow these lessons believe in practicing kindness. They believe in having respect for your elders and **ancestors**. Here are some examples. The oldest person at a table is expected to sit, drink, and eat first. This is true whether you are at home or out. South Koreans bow when they meet an older person, even a parent or grandparent. This is done to honor the person.

Think!

South Koreans celebrate a holiday called *Chuseok*. Special food is taken to **altars** at the graves of ancestors. Prayers are said for those who have died. How does this help keep the memory of ancestors alive?

Kimchi is eaten with every meal, including breakfast.

Kimchi and Sardines

Can you imagine eating something that has been buried underground for months? In South Korea, you would not only eat it. You would eat it almost every day! *Kimchi* is the name of the dish. Recipes for it are passed down in families. There are hundreds of ways to make kimchi. Most kimchi is a combination of spices and vegetables, often cabbage. It is put into large jars and buried

Jars like these store kimchi until it is ready to be eaten.

for weeks or months. Then it is dug up and served. How popular is kimchi in South Korea? It is offered in some vending machines. It has its own museum! And when South Koreans have their pictures taken, they say "kimchi!" instead of "cheese!"

Korea is almost surrounded by water. So, many favorite dishes include some type of seafood. Almost everyone eats dried, salted sardines. They are added to food the way you might add ketchup!

Traditional Korean homes look much different than homes in America.

No Shoes and Warm Floors

There are things to know before going into a South Korean's home. One of the first things you would do is take off your shoes. They are usually not allowed inside! Good manners are extremely important. For example, you should not put your feet on their furniture. You also should not pour your own drink at the table.

The Boryeong Mud Festival started in 1998.

Many people sit on the floor in their homes. There is a reason why they do this. The heating system is under the floor in most Korean homes. This is known as *ondol*. Pipes run under the floor and warm it. Many families eat, watch television, and sleep on the floor in colder weather.

Look!

Thousands of people come to South Korea every year to get really dirty. Why? They are there for the 10-day Boryeong Mud Festival. Kids enjoy the mud pool slide and the mud-land playground. Most come for the huge mud bath. Many Koreans believe the mud is good for the skin. Plus it is a lot of fun!

GLOSSARY

altars (AWL-turz) places used for religious ceremonies or prayers

ancestors (AN-ses-turz) past relatives

Buddhist (BOO-dist) followers of a man named Buddha

Confucianism (kuhn-FYOO-shuhn-iz-uhm) the belief in the teachings of a Chinese man named Confucius

Korean Words

Chuseok (CHOO-sok) South Korean holiday for honoring ancestors and family

kimchi (KIM-chi) fermented vegetables

emigrated (EM-ih-grayt-id) left your home country to live in another country

immigrants (IM-ih-gruhnts) people who have moved from one country to another and settled there

peninsula (puh-NIN-suh-luh) a section of land that is surrounded on three sides by water

ondol (OHN-dohl) system of heating homes from pipes in the floors

Ya! Ch'in-gu! (YAH! CHIN-goo!) "Hey friend!"

FIND OUT MORE

BOOKS

Bluebird Books. *Kid's Travel Journal: My Trip to South Korea.* Lulu Press, 2014.

Nelson, Carmen R. *Jacob and Katie in South Korea: The Adventures of Third Culture Kids.* Lynchburg, VA: Liberty Mountain Publishing, 2015.

Perkins, Chloe. *Living in...South Korea.* New York: Simon Spotlight, 2017.

WEBSITES

Activity Village—South Korea
https://www.activityvillage.co.uk/south-korea
Find activities and fun facts about South Korea.

Easy Science for Kids—Korea
http://easyscienceforkids.com/all-about-korea/
Here you'll find many facts and details about North and South Korea.

National Geographic Kids—South Korea
http://kids.nationalgeographic.com/explore/countries/south-korea/#south-korea-market.jpg
Read about the country's people, geography, language, and more.

INDEX

ABOUT THE AUTHOR

Tamra Orr is the author of hundreds of books for readers of all ages. She graduated from Ball State University, but moved with her husband and four children to Oregon in 2001. She is a full-time author, and when she isn't researching and writing, she writes letters to friends all over the world. Orr enjoys life in the big city of Portland and feels very lucky to be surrounded by so much diversity.